Discover *the key to* **Zero Rejection, Increased Profits,** *and* **World Class Quality**

The PROFITABLE CORRUGATED BOX CODE

Discover *the key to* **Zero Rejection, Increased Profits,** *and* **World Class Quality**

The PROFITABLE CORRUGATED BOX CODE

VISHAL & GAUGAV
MALHOTRA

Worldwide Publishing by
Pendown Press
Powered by Gullybaba.com

PENDOWN PRESS
Powered by **Gullybaba Publishing House Pvt. Ltd.,**
An ISO 9001 & ISO 14001 Certified Co.,
Regd. Office: 2525/193, 1st Floor, Onkar Nagar-A, Tri Nagar, Delhi-110035
Ph.: 09350849407, 09312235086
E-mail: info@pendownpress.com
Branch Office: 1A/2A, 20, Hari Sadan, Ansari Road, Daryaganj, New Delhi-110002
Ph.: 011-45794768
Website: PendownPress.com

First Edition: 2021

ISBN: 978-93-91544-41-6

Layout and Cover Designed by Pendown Graphics Team
Printed and bound in India by Thomson Press India Ltd.

Dedicated to our parents,
our first gurus, who taught us
the value system of staying
humble & serving society.

CONTENTS

ABOUT THE BOOK

In this book we have squeezed our 37 years of learning and provided the information in a nutshell. If you can implement the suggestions made through the book, you can tremendously improve the quality of your products and grow at a phenomenal pace. You can leave your competition far, far behind.

The book will certainly help corrugated box manufacturers like you to break the quality myths, make more money, increase profits, build reputation, and avoid common mistakes in selecting the instruments and partnering with the right vendors.

My brother and I are national award-winning testing experts with rich personal experience of 37 years. We have closely worked with multinational companies like Coca-Cola, Pepsi Co, Nestlé, Unilever, Procter & Gamble, Kellogg's, Havells, Amazon, and many more. We are both affectionately known as "Malbros" in the industry circles for our humble way of serving our partners and strongly believing in and following a customer centric approach.

INTRODUCTION

Are you raring to jump onto the bandwagon of big businesses?

Would you like to supply corrugated boxes and corrugated packaging materials to multinational companies and industry stalwarts?

Or do you constantly dream about running your corrugated boxes manufacturing plant 24 x 7 because you have received big orders from big brands.

Then this book is for you.

Why so?

What stops you from joining the big league?

It's mostly quality and standardization.

Either you don't have the correct instruments and the right know-how, or you cannot decipher how to scale your quality and standardization measures according to an increased demand.

Don't worry. This book helps you achieve both.

Every concept you have ever wanted to know. It empowers you with the information that people obtain through years of experience, in a nutshell.

Learn about what equipment to use for what types of corrugated boxes.

Learn about international standards that can immediately give you an entry into big business. Learn about compliance. Learn how to set up the perfect lab for your manufacturing facility.

Would you like to sell corrugated boxes to industry stalwarts?

Also are you wondering how can you infinite orders of big giants for your corrugated boxes…

Or may be you have a desire to run your corrugated box plant 24x7 just to meet new demands from big brands…

If you have answered Yes to any of these questions – then this book is just for you (who is an ambitious manufacturer of corrugated boxes).

Okay...

If the quality of your corrugated boxes is not assured, it doesn't just damage your shipments, it also damages your reputation irreparably. Hundreds of crores worth of items and materials are damaged or rejected because of inferior quality corrugated packaging.

The problem with corrugated boxes and packages is that sometimes it is difficult to gauge their quality by merely looking at them. They may seem premium quality, but they easily break and crack under pressure and they don't provide enough cushioning to the items contained within. By the time you realize that there is a problem, it is often too late, and the damage is done.

This is where our quality assessment technology and equipment help you.

Over the past 37 years we have helped entrepreneurs and companies save more than 2500 crores by helping them manufacture or procure corrugated boxes that are 100% reliable. How do we do it?

We provide the technology and the testing Instruments that enable our customers to manufacture or procure high quality and dependable corrugated packaging materials and boxes. Our list of esteemed customers include companies like Amazon, PepsiCo, Coca-Cola, Cadburys, Flipkart, Reckitt, Unilever, Procter & Gamble and other major national and international brands.

Who are we?

Hi. My name is Gaurav Malhotra and along with my brother Vishal Malhotra we are third-generation manufacturers of testing instruments for corrugated boxes and packaging materials.

Whenever we introduce ourselves, we like to bring into the picture the reference of the famous Wright brothers who invented the airplane. Nobody believed that man could fly. But they had the passion. They had the belief. They knew that they were on the right path. We have the same passion. Just like the Wright brothers, we single-mindedly pursue our passion of manufacturing testing instruments and help your company reach global standards.

To achieve this, we not only provide state-of-the-art instruments and the most dependable technology to our customers, but also try to educate them.

This book is a step in that direction.

Just like the Wright brothers, we are lovingly called as 'Malbros' (short for Malhotra Brothers) in the packaging industry. With our expertise, we have helped companies reach the next level of quality and save up to 22.5% within the first year itself.

The Government of India has recognized our passion and contribution for quality: Presto was honoured with the National Award for Excellent Quality, 2016-17.

There are numerous testing instruments available in the market. They either underperform or they are not utilised the way they should be. This results in low quality corrugated boxes despite investing money in the testing equipment and setting up a testing lab.

Testing equipment and testing labs for corrugated boxes are required by two categories of businesses: those who source such packaging materials from third-party manufacturers but want to make sure that the quality they get is uncompromised, or those who manufacture corrugated packaging materials and boxes themselves and want to make sure that their supplies are of an international standard and are approved by customers.

Whichever type of business you are in, you're going to find this book helpful.

CHAPTER 1

WHY TESTING YOUR CORRUGATED PACKAGING AND BOXES IS NON-NEGOTIABLE?

If you deal with corrugated packaging and boxes, you face rejections from your customers through two quarters:

Rejection of the packaging material itself if you are a manufacturer of corrugated boxes and packaging materials.

Rejection of your product due to faulty or inferior quality packaging.

Rejections by your customers don't just drill holes into your bottom line, they are also bad for your reputation.

But do you know that there is a possibility of zero rejections of your products as far as your corrugated packaging is concerned?

Just imagine what wonders your zero-rejection rate can work on your reputation and brand. You can become a leader in your industry!

This is not just speculation. We have been helping our customers achieve zero rejections (concerning corrugated packaging) or minimize the rejections, for more than three decades. We have an unblemished track record.

Do you know that every year, out of 100 companies in the corrugated packaging industry, 29 are new – they have just started in the current year.

Do you also know that 12 companies out of every existing 100 companies in the corrugated packaging industry are forced to shut their shop?

It shows that this industry is in a constant flux. New companies are coming, and old companies are closing down.

It shows that there is great demand in the corrugated packaging industry but surviving in this industry is quite difficult.

The lack of quality testing is one of the biggest culprits.

To survive and to grow, you need to remain ahead of the curve by maintaining world-class quality and by optimizing your production.

Given below is a small, real-world example.

A previously successful packaging company from Chennai contacted us. They were feeling the heat of the competition. Their profits were dipping. They were on the verge of shutting down one of their plants.

Based on our testing and equipment, we recommended a simple change. It was found that they were using a higher grammage (GSM) paper than what was required for their type of packaging needs.

They reduced the grammage immediately, and to their great delight, were able to save 3.5 crores in less than a year. Instead of closing the plant, they had turned profitable within a year. They invested in a new lab to make testing an integral part of their entire manufacturing process.

It was indeed a happy moment for us when their owner came with a box of sweets and invited us to the inauguration of their new plant. This was just a few months after they were contemplating closing one of the existing plants!

Here is another success story facilitated by our testing equipment and lab facilities…

A small manufacturer of corrugated boxes wanted to become a vendor of a huge multinational. He had been trying to get the contract for many years but with little success.

Then, one day, while visiting the client, by chance he saw our Bursting Strength Tester that the client was using to test the quality and durability of their packaging material that they were sourcing from other vendors. He realized why he wasn't getting the contract from the multinational: the quality of his corrugated boxes was being rejected by the testing standards of the company.

He noted down the phone number that was present on the equipment and contacted us. He sought our help to improve his quality.

We suggested he buy only a few pieces of equipment in the beginning. We also helped him establish a lab for his manufacturing facility.

He was hesitant to establish a lab because he thought that the lab would not increase his production in any way. However, he knew that he needed to raise the standard of his production to land a contract with the multinational. So, he invested in instruments.

He tested the materials using his new equipment and offered a sample free of cost to the multinational company, along with the test reports and the picture of the wonderful new lab.

The senior executives at the multinational company could not believe that he could achieve such good quality. Just to double check, they visited his factory for inspection, validation and then, subsequent approval.

Now he is one of their biggest and the most preferred suppliers, and he has turned an ardent believer of consistently measuring the quality of his corrugated boxes.

Quality mustn't be compromised. At the same time, lowering your production costs is also essential in the face of growing competition. Fortunately, both can be achieved with our equipment and lab facilities. By optimizing quality and minimizing costs, coupled with zero rejections, you will not only survive in this highly competitive field of corrugated boxes and packaging, but you will also grow. Make quality assessment an integral part of the corrugated box manufacturing and packaging process.

A common mistake that can be easily avoided

We encountered Mr. RD Sharma who is a corrugated box manufacturer in North India. His huge shipment of boxes got rejected as the bursting strength was not up to the standards set by the customer. Lots of discussion and heated debates went on between him and the customer. The point of contention was that when he was testing his boxes through the instruments set up at his place the bursting strength was coming to be acceptable, but the same was failing the test on the customer's side.

He visited the lab of the customer and contacted us since the instrument being used by the customer was ours. He wanted to know why there was a difference.

He wanted us to check his machine that he had bought from a local company at a low price just a few months ago. Upon his repeated requests, we sent a team to investigate the matter.

Our team was astonished to find that although the machine seemed like ours, upon checking closely, they found that the hydraulic system movement of the plunger was causing more glycerin to flow, which resulted in a higher bursting strength than the actual. Even the rubber diaphragm did not meet the Shore A value specified in the standard and was flexing more.

Then the team verified results with a calibrated master and saw that the instrument was giving inaccurate readings.

Mr. Sharma had saved a few thousand rupees by purchasing a low-quality machine in the short run for sure, but had lost a few lakhs of material, his brand value, and a good client who would have given him long-term profits.

Please remember that the quality assurance instruments shouldn't be bought as an afterthought. They are actually meant to give you accurate results, help you improve your quality, and finally, grow your business by delivering a zero-rejection rate.

CHAPTER 2

THREE TYPES OF TESTING INSTRUMENTS THAT EVERY LAB MUST HAVE

Just as one shoe does not fit all, one instrument cannot fulfil all your corrugated package testing needs. The testing instruments in the corrugated industry can be categorized into three separate sections:

- Strength testing
- Transport worthiness
- Physical properties

One of the primary reasons why we are writing this book is that we want to help the readers choose the right instruments for their quality testing needs. There are many vendors out there who misguide you in choosing the wrong instruments for their petty gains. This chapter helps you make the right decisions. If you follow the guidelines, you will not end up buying instruments that will give you the wrong results.

In this chapter we have included a table that gives you all the details that you need to save lakhs of rupees when buying only those instruments that you need, and nothing more. Presented here are two real-world examples just to illustrate how important it is to buy the right instruments.

Mr. SK Arora, a box manufacturer from UP, was misguided by local suppliers and on their advice, he ended up buying two separate bursting strength testers – one for paper and the other for corrugated boxes – on the pretext that only this combination could give accurate results. Heeding to their advice, Mr. Arora bought both the testers. Later, when he met us at an exhibition, we told him that there was no need to purchase separate instruments for testing the bursting strength of paper and corrugated boxes. Both could be achieved by a single instrument, which is the norm worldwide.

He found it hard to believe. We advised him to do a simple search on Google and the results that he found amazed him.

This is one reason we want to educate the people in the industry.

Here is another example.

Mr. Anand from an export house was similarly misguided by a supplier to invest in a double head bursting strength tester – one for paper and another for corrugated boxes. This is not an international norm. We invited Mr. Anand over to our in-house laboratory for a free testing of his paper and corrugated board samples on a single head machine with dual checkpoints (high & low).

He was astonished to see the accurate results as per the expectations. He bought a single instrument from us instead of two instruments. He saved money as well as space in the laboratory. The testing became easier for the lab in-charge too.

Here is the table we had mentioned above. It acts as a ready reckoner to help you decide the right instruments for your lab.

S No.	Instrument	Usage	Relevant Standards	Space Requirement	Electrical Requirement
1	Bursting Strength Tester Digital	Paper, Cardboard, Corrugated boxes, Leather, Fabrics, Plastic films, Plastic sheet, Foils etc.	ASTM D 3786-01, ASTM D 3786 – 80A, ISO 1060 PART-1 1987.	540 (W) X 600 (D) X 600 (H) mm	220 V ac +/- 10 V, 50 Hz, 15 A
2	Bursting Strength Tester Pnuematic	Paper, Cardboard, Corrugated boxes, Leather, Fabrics, Plastic films, Plastic sheet, Foils etc.	ASTM D 3786-01, ASTM D 3786 – 80A, ISO 1060 PART-1 1987.	540(W)X 600(D) X 600(H) mm	220 V ac +/- 10 V, 50 Hz, 15 A

3	Box Compression Tester 1000x1000 mm	Corrugated Boxes	ASTM D642, ASTM D4169, TAPPI T804, ISO 12048, and JIS Z0212	1670(W) X 1080(D) X1900(H) mm	220 V ac +/- 10 V, 50 Hz, 15 A
4	Box Compression Tester 600x600mm	Corrugated Boxes	ASTM D642, ASTM D4169, TAPPI T804, ISO 12048, and JIS Z0213	1050(W)X 650(D) X 650(H) mm	220 V ac +/- 10 V, 50 Hz, 15 A
5	Box Compression Tester -Mini 200x200mm	Printed/ non printed Monocarton boxes	TAPPI T-804/ ISO 12048/ ASTM D-642	600(W)X 455(D) X 830(H) mm	220 V ac +/- 10 V, 50 Hz, 10 A
6	Drop Tester Hand Operated Manual	Corrugated Boxes, Containers, Plastic bottles, Sacks, Bags	ASTM D5276-98	1250(W)X 1050(D)X 1950(H) mm	NA
7	Drop Tester Motorized Operated	Corrugated Boxes, Containers, Plastic bottles, Sacks, Bags	ASTM D5276-99	1550(W) X 1350(D) X 1950(H) mm	220 V ac +/- 10 V, 50 Hz, 10 A
8	Edge Crush Tester -ECT/ RCT	Corrugated Sheets, Paper	IS 7063, ISO 3037-2013: Tappi T-811	600(W) X 500(D) X 500(H) mm	220 V ac +/- 10 V, 50 Hz, 5 A
9	Puncture Tester	Cardboards	TAPPI –T803, ISO 3036 and ASTM D781	720(W) X 455(D) X 720(H) mm	220 V ac +/- 10 V, 50 Hz, 5 A
10	Moisture Meter	Cardboards, Papers, Fabrics, Leather, Wood	Measuring Instrument	Portable approx. 250 X 250 mm	NA,Battery operated
11	Scuff Tester	Printed plastic films, Printed monocartons, Labels, Stickers	ASTM F2497-05, BS 3110:1959	420(W) X 550(D) X 680(H) mm	220 V ac +/- 10 V, 50 Hz, 5 A

12	GSM Cutter	Fabric, Plastic film, Paper, Corrugated sheet	ASTM D646 - 96 ; Tappi T410 OM-08	Portable approx. 130 X130 mm	NA
13	GSM Balance	Fabric, Plastic film, Paper, Corrugated sheet	Measuring Instrument	300 X300 mm	220 V ac +/- 10 V, 50 Hz, 5 A
14	Ink abrasion Tester	Labels, Folding cartons, Corrugated boxes, Circulars, and other Packaging materials having applied graphics on a flat substrate	ASTM 5264-98	300(W) X 428(D) X 470(H) mm	220 V ac +/- 10 V, 50 Hz, 5 A
15	Colour Matching Cabinet	Plastic, Painting, Plating, Paper, and Textile	CIE International Standards	670(W) X 572(D) X 616(H) mm	220 V ac +/- 10 V, 50 Hz, 5 A
16	Colorimeter	Plastic, Painting, Plating, Paper, and textile	CIE International Standards	Portable 205(W) X 80(D) X 70(H) mm	220 V ac +/- 10 V, 50 Hz, 5 A
17	Vibration Table	Filled shipping containers/ packages	ASTM D999, TAPPI T-17, IS 7028 (part II)	840(W) X 840(D) X 980(H) mm	220 V ac +/- 10 V, 50 Hz, 15 A
18	Tearing Tester	Paper, Fabrics, Plastic films	ASTM D1424-09(2013), ASTM D624-00(2012), ASTM D1776, ASTM D689	450(W) X 275(D) X 530(H) mm	NA
19	COBB Value	Paper, Fabrics, Carrugated Sheets	IS 1060, TAPPI –T441	350(W) X 140(D) X 230(H) mm	NA
20	Thickness Gauge -Micron	Plastic films, Plastic sheets, Fabrics,	Measuring Instrument	Portable	NA, Battery operated

CHAPTER 3

KNOW ALL THE STANDARDS THAT MATTER THE MOST

For every product, every country and every industry has their own standards. Some examples include TAPPI, ISTA, ASTM, DIN, JIS, IS, and many more. These standards are defined so that the instruments and the testing procedures can be standardized, and consistently uniform results can be achieved whether a particular product is being tested in India or any other country. This is done to ensure repeatability and reliability as well as the standardization of the tests.

Here is an example of what happens when standards are not followed or when an equipment is used that is not standardized:

The test standards for the same instrument may vary from country to country. For example, the test height may vary from 500 mm to 1800 mm for different standards in a Drop Test.

Imagine dropping a box from a height of 500 mm and marking it as "PASS" and then shipping it, but getting the box rejected by the buyer because he follows a different standard and tests the drop from a height of 1500 mm. If a consistent standard is followed when testing the box, the right height will be used at both the ends.

Along with knowing the importance of following the standards, you also need to ensure that the equipment that you are purchasing allows you to follow the standards. Here is another example…

A customer started comparing the price of a vibration table that was 50% cheaper than what we were quoting him. We were intrigued by the price disparity and wanted to get to the root of this. When we closely checked the specifications, we observed that the cheaper vibration table did not meet the requirements of the ASTM D 999 and IS 7028 standards as required by the client. The frequency was fixed and not variable which was again required by the standards. The angle of the swivel could not be altered. The customer would have wasted his money in buying the wrong non-standard instrument had we not educated him.

It is always prudent to buy testing instruments from reputed manufacturers who are technically sound. These manufacturers understand both national and international standards as well as how they can impact your business. Remember that you don't just buy an instrument, you buy the experience and the value that instrument delivers.

CHAPTER 4

THE MISSING INGREDIENTS THAT PROMISE CONSISTENT RESULTS

What is the state of chaos? A state of chaos is where there is no order. Everything is random. Imagine a cricket team where nobody listens to the captain and every player does what he wishes to do. Fielders randomly go stand in the field and the bowlers bowl in whichever manner they want to bowl. Can that team ever win? No chance.

Exactly this is what happens when people are setting up testing laboratories without giving much thought to standards to be followed and the results to be obtained. The same tests give different results.

What's missing here? Keep guessing.

While we are guessing, let's explore another story. Recently we helped a multinational set up multiple labs across the country at their different plants. We supplied all the instruments for their labs. These instruments were world class and standardized. Were they happy with the results? No.

The results were not consistent and were completely out of control. They were getting into regular disputes with their vendors because the results never tallied. The vendors would come up with higher values than the ones being tested at our multinational's labs. Even the results between the labs of the multinational's own plants didn't match!

We were made to run from one lab to another (in different cities) exploring issues with the instruments and trying to analyze problems that did not exist. After a month of exploration and analysis, we discovered the missing ingredient. Guess again...

It was...

SOP (Standard Operating Practices)

Or rather, the lack of them.

Once we had zeroed in on the problem, we made the multinational company create standard operating practices and the results were mind blowing. The disparities between their results and the results of their vendors immediately vanished. The results became consistent between their labs and the testing facilities of their vendors. Our reward was of course the satisfaction and happiness on their faces.

We would similarly want you to experience the benefits of establishing standard operating practices and then turn profitable. We hope that with quality equipment and standardized labs, there is greater peace in your life and there are zero, or at least minimal disputes between your suppliers and customers.

Why is it important to establish a standardized methodology for conducting and performing tests? Even if you have the best instruments, if you don't set the benchmarks, if you don't establish a uniform environment for comparison, it is like the above-mentioned cricket team. Nobody knows who is doing what? When you don't follow a standardized procedure, you don't know what values to check against or 'compare with'? You cannot document which materials perform the best under which parameters.

Want your team to win the match? Read on...

Why do you need to establish standard operating practices at your organization?

Practice and training are important, but they are not the ultimate solutions. These activities do not guarantee efficient and smooth workflows in an organization.

A set of SOPs on the other hand, will ensure that you have a well-structured quality system and a set of procedures that introduce an environment of uniformity and consistency across the board.

Clearly defining SOPs delivers you the following benefits:

- **Process consistency:** When an individual or a group of individuals knows how they are supposed to perform a certain task and what results to expect, they know the benchmark. There will be fewer conflicts. There will be greater synergy.
- **Elimination of errors:** A standard procedure gives you a set of predefined instructions to perform a particular task. It is like a roadmap. Everyone knows where to start and where to end. This reduces or eliminates errors.

- **Better communication:** Standard operating practices do away with the need to train staff repeatedly. Once you have a clearly defined set of SOPs, there is a common understanding between all the departments and branches, and even among all the customers, clients and vendors.
- **Time-saving:** Making changes and alterations or processing rejections can be time-consuming. In the presence of SOPs, there is a uniformity of expectations. You know what you're delivering and the other party knows what it is getting. There are few rejections and fewer demands for improvisation. This saves you a lot of time and money.
- **Organizational welfare:** With greater sense of consistency and synergy, there are fewer or no conflicts. Instead of firefighting and problem solving, your employees spend their time being productive. With fewer conflicts and rejections, you establish a strong brand presence. Your reputation in the industry improves. There is better growth and profitability. You maintain a healthy environment.
- **Better standards compliance:** It is assumed that you will be creating your standard operating practices based on global compliance standards. Once these SOPs are defined and communicated across the board, compliance becomes automatic and there are zero digressions.
- **Improved accountability:** Once you have a set of standard operating practices, your managers know how to evaluate the overall performance of the staff and

the products because they have the yardstick. Employees can be rewarded and held accountable according to their performance because now their individual performance is easily manageable.

- **Consistency:** Since all your production processes and lab testing conditions are laid out in the standard operating practices, there is consistency across the board. The staff knows what results are expected and all the processes are defined towards those expectations. This delivers consistent results.
- **Organizational proficiency:** Since your entire staff and equipment are working with synchronicity due to an environment of uniformity introduced by your SOPs, the overall proficiency within the organization improves. The results are as expected, which leads to better forecasting and resource management.
- **A guiding force:** The set of standing operating practices also acts as a guiding force for all the employees. It becomes a mandatory document that all the employees must internalize for optimal performance. This helps them stay on course and strive towards the common organizational goals.

DOCUMENT CONTROL SOP TEMPLATE		
SOP NO.	AUTHOR	DATE
PROCEDURE NAME		
PROPOSE	Describe who the SOP is for and why it is necessary.	
SCOPE	Describe the type of documents to be included in a version control system.	
RESPONSIBILITIES	Detail who will maintain the document system and this SOP.	
VERSION CONTROL PROCEDURES	Describe your naming, numbering and dating conventions for your document. Include details of page and document formatting conventions. Add a graphic example to the procedure or as an appendix, any differences between convention for each type of document.	
ARCHIVING CONVENTION	Describe how and when documents are archived.	
REFERENCES	List any referral documents, if required.	

Since we are talking in detail about defining a set of SOPs for your organization (in the context of this book, for measuring corrugated boxes and packages), we thought of sharing a document template that can help you organize the various aspects of your standard operating practices. You can refer to the above image for visual reference.

Contents of an ideal SOP document

- **Title section:** The title section uniquely identifies the SOP name. This section may contain, aside from the practice name, a unique ID, the author's name, and the date of creation.

- **Purpose:** This section describes the purpose of the SOP so that the employees referring to it know why the SOP was created.
- **Scope:** Which parts of the measurement are to be included.
- **Responsibilities:** Which employees and managers are responsible for ensuring that the measurements adhere to the scope of this document.
- **Version control:** How are different versions of the SOP document to be implemented, and if changes are to be made in future, how they will be made.
- **Archiving conventions:** In case this particular practice document is not needed, how is it to be archived?
- **References:** Any reference documents used for the purpose of creating the SOP document.
- **Health and safety warnings:** Any precautions to be taken when taking the measurements.
- **Approval signatures:** The signatories who have reviewed the SOP document and approved it.

SIMPLE SOP TEMPLATE			
SOP NO.	AUTHOR	DATE	ISSUE
TITLE			
EXAMPLE TITLE			
BACKGROUND			
SOP INTRODUCTION			
IF IN DOUBT-ASK!!!		PAGE	

CHAPTER 5

CHECKLIST FOR SELECTING THE RIGHT INSTRUMENTS

Your products are accepted or rejected based on their quality. Nonetheless, it is tragic that most business owners pay the least attention to the testing facilities. The primary focus is on selecting the right production machines (of course, that's important), or increasing their sales (also important).

Scientific quality testing is mostly an afterthought. They prefer to get the feedback from their friends, some randomly chosen consultants, or by advising their purchase team to obtain the cheapest equipment available in the market.

Just as production machinery is needed to produce corrugated boxes and packaging materials, the right instruments are needed to make sure that your boxes and materials comply with international standards and provide the durability expected by the customers. If the quality is compromised, if standardization is not implemented, no matter how much material you manufacture, it is of no use – it is going to get rejected or your customers are quietly going to move to other providers without even informing you what the problem is.

Often, the purchase team goes out with a single mission get 2-3 quotes and then finalise the cheapest instruments with favourable credit terms. They don't realize that by not giving highest priority to the testing instruments, they are causing immense harm to their business. The selection of testing equipment and instruments for the lab should never be taken lightly.

Before you invest in your laboratory instruments, they need to be evaluated, checked and verified for reliability, accuracy, consistency, and repeatability. Talk about these terms with your purchase team and you will draw a blank. "Boss, what are you asking???" they will exclaim.

Don't worry though. We are writing this book because we want to help you set up the most well-equipped laboratory for quality testing that will bring your rejection rate to zero, or bring it as low as humanly possible.

It is always easier to go through a checklist. When you have a checklist, you can be sure that you are not missing anything because as you check the various points that you must keep in mind when buying instruments for your testing lab, you can tick them off.

Given below is a checklist that we have prepared for you. We have combined years of experience and feedback that we have obtained from various manufacturers and customers to prepare this all-encompassing checklist. You can take a printout if you like and keep it in front of you when you are inspecting equipment before purchasing it.

Checklist for selecting the right instruments

Sr. No.	Instrument	Must have features
1	Bursting Strength Tester – Digital	•High & low selectable range of testing. •Memory to hold up to 9 test readings. •Strong gripping clamps. •Grooved structure of the test specimen holder to avoid slippage and keep the specimen being tested in place. •Inbuilt calibration facility. •Bright LED display. •Feather touch controls. •Calibration lock. •Key features certificate with NABL traceability. •Wiring diagram. •Spares accessories.
2	Bursting Strength Tester – Pneumatic	•High & low selectable range of testing. •Memory to hold up to 9 test readings. •Auto sample locking under selectable pressure ranges. •Ability to adjust clamping pressure. •Inbuilt calibration facility. •Bright LED display. •Feather touch controls. •Calibration lock. •Key features certificate with NABL traceability. •Wiring diagram. •Spares accessories.
3	Box Compression Tester 1000 x 1000 mm	•Highly accurate test results under uniform compression force. •TARE and peak hold facility. •Over travel protection. •Inbuilt calibration facility. •Fast runner option. •Feather touch controls. •Permanent laser marking grooves provided for correct placement of the test specimen. • Key feature certificate with NABL traceability. •Wiring diagram.

4	Box Compression Tester 600 x 600 mm	Highly accurate test results under uniform compression force. •TARE and peak hold facility. •Over travel protection. •Inbuilt calibration facility. •Fast runner option. •Feather touch controls. •Permanent laser marking grooves provided for correct placement of the test specimen. • Key feature certificate with NABL traceability. •Wiring diagram.
5	Box Compression Tester – mini 200 x 200 mm	•Inbuilt calibration facility. •Direct digital readout of compression strength and deflection. •Provision for faster speed for approach and return to the top of the specimen. •Sophisticated electronic controls for precision and easy operation. •TARE and peak hold facility. •Over travel protection. •Overload protection. •Certificate with NABL traceability. •Wiring diagram.
6	Drop Tester – hand operated (manual)	•Ability to raise the test platform by a guiding mechanism. •Drop height adjustable clamp. •Straight and angular drop tests can be performed on a single instrument. •Strong base plate with a rugged structure.
7	Drop Test – motorized	•Ability to raise the test platform by a guided motorized mechanism. •Drop height adjustable clamp. •Straight and angular drop tests can be performed on a single instrument. •Strong base plate with rugged structure. •Electric hoist for positioning drop assembly and lifting heavy packages. •Dropping operations through pneumatic system. •Certificate with NABL traceability. •Wiring diagram.

8	Edge Crush Tester – ECT/RCT 	•Microprocessor-based display for accurate test results. •Separate fixtures for ring crush, edge crush and flat crush test along with measuring templates. •Highly accurate test results under compression force. •Inbuilt calibration facility. •Feather touch controls. •Certificate with NABL traceability. •Wiring diagram.
9	Puncture Tester 	•High quality rugged structure with corrosion resistant main body. •Display for impact/absorbed energy and angle of test specimen. •Single-handed, hassle-free operation. •Highly accurate test results and the impact forces. •Ability to test under different energy weights. •Puncture head collar with soft adjustment to puncture head base. •Inbuilt calibration facility. •Certificate with NABL traceability. •Wiring diagram.
10	Moisture Meter 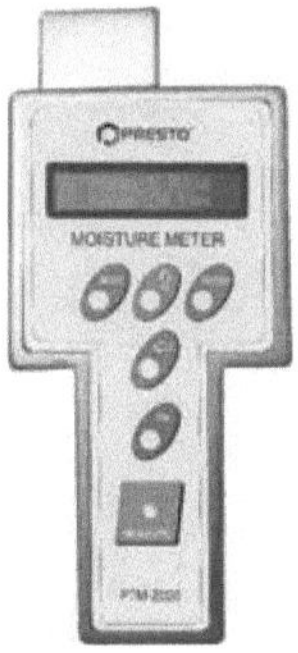	•Clear digital LCD display. •Microprocessor-based circuit. •Moisture range for paper: 4%-18.2% and for baled scrap paper: 6%-40%. •Selection of paper types: 3. •Setting of tolerance limits for pass/fail. •Average of up to 100 readings display. •Data storage: Max 300 readings (100 per paper type). •Inbuilt calibration facility. •Battery saving mode. •Auto power off.

11	Scuff Tester 	•Uniform load by weights on test sample for even testing. •Ability to set number of counts through a digital preset counter. •Motorized gear system for scuff movement. •Digital counter that can be set up to 9999 counts. •Highly accurate and precise results under uniform load and rubbing clamp movement. •Certificate with NABL traceability. •Wiring diagram. •Spares accessories.
12	GSM Cutter 	•High-quality aluminum pressure die casted main body. •Lightweight and resilient. •Highly accurate test results. •Heavy duty German cutting blades. •Available with safety latch. •Spares accessories.
13	GSM Balance 	•Compact windshield with the scale. •Precise and air free weighing due to breeze shield. •Complete supply with inspection. •Calibration certificate. •Specially designed to determine the GSM of paper and packaging.
14	Ink Rub Tester 	•Equipped with high-end microprocessor to control testing with frequency of rubbing with controlled load. •Even load distribution on rubbing areas of sample ensured. •Noise free rubbing process. •Two different load weights. •Certificate with NABL traceability. •Wiring diagram.
15	Colour Matching Cabinet 	•Standardized and controlled lighting conditions. •Wide viewing area. •High-quality light sources. •Comes with 5 light sources as per the CIE international standards.

16	Colorimeter 	•Adopts an accurate camera locating feature. •Illuminated locating for user's ease of operation. •Software-based output of test results. •Auto white and black calibration. •Display of whiteness, yellowness and colour fastness. •Convenient operation and ergonomic design. •Small measuring aperture-easy to measure concave-convex objects. •Creative facula locating and cross locating.
17	Vibration Table 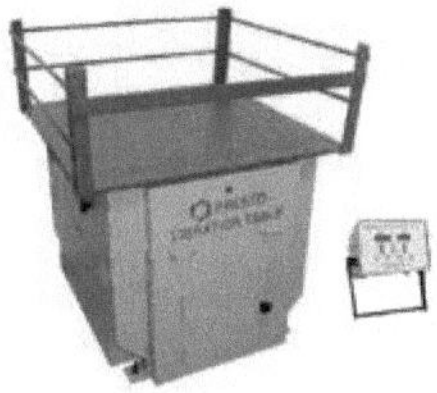	•Highly accurate test results under various frequency settings. •Digital timer for setting test run time. •Sample slippage protection by rail on all sides. •Strong base plate with rugged structure. •Adjustable frequency. •Vertical and swivel modes of vibration.
18	Tearing Tester 	•Falling pendulum -type instrument. •Single-handed hassle-free operation. •Highly accurate test results under multiple pendulum weights. •Strong gripping fixture for holding test samples. •Pendulum release mechanism to cover various measuring ranges. •Inbuilt calibration weights.
19	COBB Value 	•High quality rugged structure with corrosion resistant main body. •Lightweight and resilient. •Fast locking mechanism. •Single-handed hassle-free operation. •Highly accurate test results. •High-grade stainless steel test area.

20	Thickness Gauge-micron 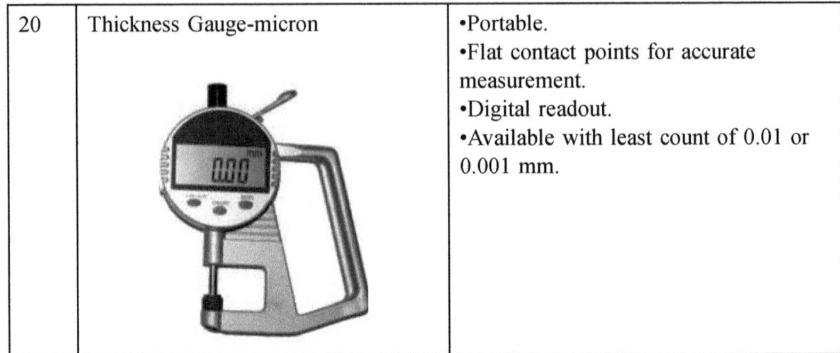	•Portable. •Flat contact points for accurate measurement. •Digital readout. •Available with least count of 0.01 or 0.001 mm.

CHAPTER 6

THE 1-PAGE MAGICAL REPORT

By now, let's assume that you have got the best instruments from the best supplier. You also have the best standard operating practices in place. But what about reports? Are you still preparing your reports on plain sheets of paper or even MS Excel?

The efficacy of every system ultimately depends on reporting. How the data is organized, how it is interpreted and how it is archived for future references – these are as important as obtaining the correct data.

Let's say it is equivalent to making the best dishes but not presenting them in an appetizing manner.

There are two reasons why you need professionally designed impeccable reports: they help to analyze the results in an efficient manner, and they also help you make a good impression on your customers and business partners when your corrugated boxes and packages are accompanied by the informative and well laid out test reports.

Also, through systematic archiving, you can prepare a consolidated database of all your reports generated so far. Once you have built your database, you can categorize information based on vendors, products and their dimensions, quality outcomes, and time periods, just to name a few possibilities. Up till now, only the large commercial labs have had access to such reporting capabilities.

What does a typical report contain? Below we have described the various headers and columns:

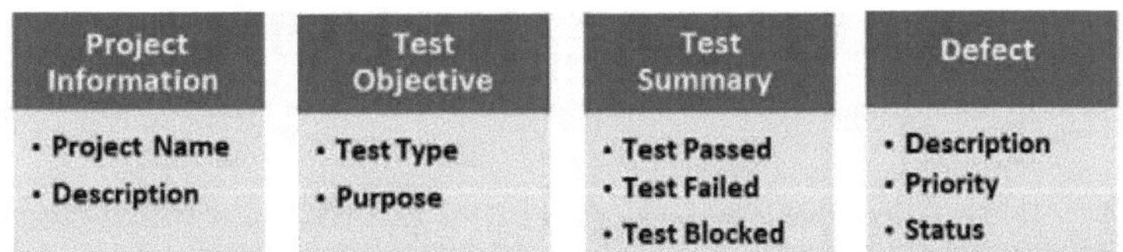

Here is an elaboration

Project Information: This column can have the information that helps you identify the project such as the project or the product name, the batch number, the material being tested, the employee's name carrying out the test, the standard against which the test is being done, and other descriptions.

Test Objective

What the test aims to achieve or achieves. This comes in the planning stage, but it can be included in the report to get some perspective. You can include information such as test type, the desired results, units of measurement, test performance, nature of tests, and so on.

Test Summary

This is the gist of the test which very well defines your report. It may contain a tabular section for a graphical representation containing the summary of test results at a glance. The various outcomes may include–

- No. of tests performed.
- No. of tests passed.
- No. of tests failed.
- Passed percentage.
- Failed percentage.
- Tabular and graphical representation of different sets of parameters.
- User comments.

The test summary can also contain information distinguished by color indicators, graphs, and tables.

You can display metrics such as buckling failure, compressive stress, and compressive strain, just to give you a few examples.

Below is an example of color-coded graphical representation of various outcomes.

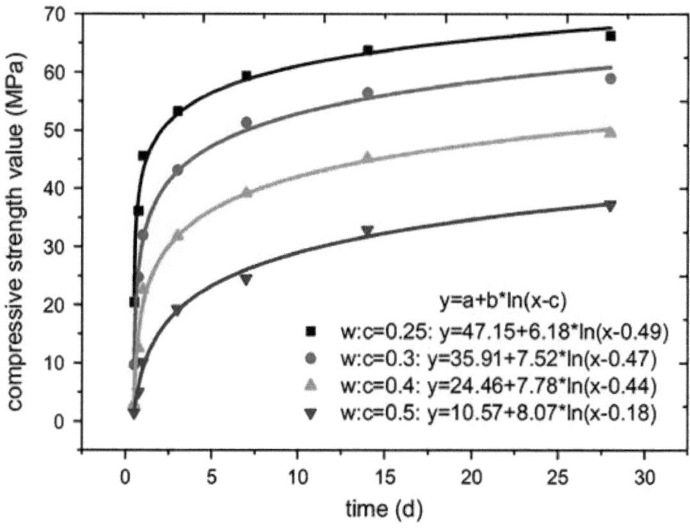

Reports are not normally uniform. The format and the information contained within different reports may vary according to the purpose or the intention of the test and the operational steps needed to get optimal results. But most of the reports contain the following bits of information that remain more or less consistent:

- Information about the test procedure along with test methods based on the selected standard.
- The lab atmospheric conditions.
- The description of the material or the product being tested.
- The dimension and the shape of the test piece and the nature and the area of the surface being tested.
- The information about how the material has been prepared before testing, such as the cleaning treatment applied, and any protection given to the edges and other special areas.
- The number of pieces tested from each material and product.
- The percentage of pass/failure of the samples during the test.
- The duration of the test and the results of any intermediate inspections.
- Any abnormality or incident occurring during the entire test process.
- Intervals between different inspections.
- Time and date of the test.
- Photographic records of the tested pieces can also accompany the report.

The 1-page magical report

SAMPLE TEST REPORT		DATE: 03 / 07 / 2020		TIME: 11:03 AM	
MACHINE NAME: TENSILE TESTING MACHINE (CAP. : 50 KGF.) DIGITAL MODEL : ATTM 50					
COMPANY NAME: GLOCOT CHEMICALS PVT. LTD					
Address: 45, HSIDC INDUSTRIAL AREA, RAI SONIPAT 131029		Video: https://vimeo.com/434958607 /5ca7689bc9			
SAMPLE ID	PRESSAMP015		OPERATOR NAME		SARITA NEGI
LOT NO.	12		SAMPLE LENGTH		115 MM
BATCH NO.	4		SAMPLE WIDTH		6 MM
PRODUCT NAME	RUBBER SAMPLE		SAMPLE THICKNESS		3.01 MM
TEST SPEED	50 & 500 MM/MIN		SHAPE/GSM		DUMBBELL
SAMPLE	**NO.1**	**NO.2**	**NO.3**	**NO.4**	**NO.5**
YES	0.960 / 216 MM (500 MM/MIN) kgf	0.860 / 200 MM (50 MM/MIN) kgf	--	--	--
	Elongation kgf	Elongation kgf	Elongation --	Elongation --	Elongation --
Testing Instructions :					
QC Remarks : Sample tested with 50 kgf capacity TTM, would advice to purchase TTM having load cell capacity 10 kgf with least count 1 g .					
Disclaimer : *Testing procedures were performed to the best of our ability. Reports/certificates or any attachments shall NOT be reproduced, these are complimentary free of cost tests done solely to support the client in making an informed instrument buying decision . Reports relate ONLY to the samples tested and are issued in good faith and cannot be used for legal purposes or disputes settlement .*					

CHECKED BY:
Sarita Negi

www.prestogroup.com

info@prestogroup.com

How to prepare an ethical test report?

Your test report represents how your corrugated boxes and packing materials are going to fare. Upon these boxes and packaging materials depend the safety and security of the items enclosed within. Your customers put their stake in your packaging based on your test reports. Therefore, it is vital that you make sure that all the standards are met, and all the data is well represented in the report.

CHAPTER 7

WHAT YOUR VENDOR DOES NOT WANT YOU TO KNOW & HOW TO SELECT THE RIGHT VENDOR

The digital world can be misleading. It is also true that whenever you're looking for information on corrugated testing materials and equipment for your lab, you visit some fancy websites. Most of these websites are made to lure and fool you into investing your hard-earned money and buy instruments and services from unreliable sources.

Do you really want to become such an easy target for these fly-by-night operators? No, we don't think so.

Here is a story of one of our customers who got swayed by a fancy website that claimed that they had "global offices". Their salespeople were smooth talkers, and they offered a deal that was too good to be true. Nonetheless, the customer, Mr. Naik, bought the equipment because they had agreed to take part payment after installation.

The ordeal began immediately. The instrument that was supposed to be delivered within four weeks, was delivered after four months and that too, after extensive following up. The piece was totally different from what was displayed on the website. The colour was different. The design fell short of his expectations. The instrument didn't even fully perform the functions that it was supposed to perform.

The vendor never asked for the balance payment because by delivering such a lousy piece they had already made a profit in the initial stage.

They stopped picking up the phone. All the smooth talking after-sales service was gone. All that money went down the drain.

It makes us sad to see unsuspecting companies falling prey to such unscrupulous traders simply because these companies think that they are getting a good deal and they can save some money.

The instruments are offered cheap, the websites are fancy, and before you have bought and made the payment, they make you feel as if you're the most important customer they have ever had.

Do you want to find a good vendor for your testing lab?

No, there is no need to depend on trial and error.

Through our extensive experience, we have prepared a checklist. Given below is a list of questions & pointers you should ask before settling with a vendor. In 99% of the cases, you will be able to make the right choice and save yourself a ton of money as well as time.

- How much experience does a vendor have in providing testing instruments in the corrugated packaging industry?

- Are they manufacturers or traders? Make sure you verify this fact. Check their factory license. Request them to show the video of the factory with the company name prominently displayed.
- Visit their factory and check their quality parameters.
- Take your samples and ask them to test them in front of you. If a physical visit is not possible, ask them to do it through Zoom, WhatsApp video or Google Meet.
- Try to contact the existing customers over phone or through a personal visit.
- Does your vendor have a service setup? Do they have in-house engineers working for them or do they outsource the servicing jobs? Ask for ESI/PF records of the engineers.
- Do they have in-house calibration masters? If yes, check their certifications.
- What is the condition of their spare parts inventory? In case you experience a breakdown, will they be able to provide you the needed spare parts promptly along with service support?
- Beware of traders; they will buy from anywhere and supply you the equipment with maximum margin for themselves. They may not even provide you the needed backup, after sale service and spare parts.
- Does the vendor have a CRM in place? Whom will you call in case there is trouble?

CONCLUSION

This brings us to the end of the book, and we have really enjoyed sharing the crux of our knowledge with you. We really hope the book has been able to deliver value to you and help you in deciding the equipment to invest in and whom to partner with for your lab needs.

So, what is the next step? What should you do to make sure that all your corrugated boxes and packaging testing needs are fulfilled according to international standards?

You have got two choices: continue the way you have been doing business so far. Depend on trial and error. Expect a miracle. Let chance be at the driving seat.

The other choice is that use the knowledge contained within this book and then put it to some good use. Partner with a world-class company to build your testing lab. Improve your quality. Raise your standards. Attain zero rejection rate. Increase your profits. Join the league of world-class companies. Achieve your potential.

No, this is not just pep talk.

In the beginning of this book, we mentioned why many businesses in the corrugated industry need to shut shop because they cannot meet the quality standards and even if they try to maintain a certain sense of quality, they're not investing in the right equipment.

Hence, if you can improve your quality standards and if you can meet the quality guidelines of your customers, there is no reason for you to not attain great success.

You know what's best for your business, and we know what's the best way to test your corrugated boxes and packaging materials. My brother and I are third-generation manufacturers of testing instruments for labs. This is what we have grown up doing. Our testing lab instruments and equipment are being used by multinational companies such as Amazon, Pepsi Co, Cadburys, Coca-Cola, Procter & Gamble, and many more.

We know that the quality that you attain can make or break your business. In that realm our commitment is uncompromising and unwavering.

If you want to discuss further with us, feel free to connect through **info@prestogroup.com** and we will gladly provide you all the needed information.

You can also browse our website **https://prestogroup.com**– we have been trying our best to make it into a treasure trove of knowledge and information. Of course, you can always call us.

Got any questions about the book?

Feel free to contact.

9 789391 544416

Printed by Libri Plureos GmbH in Hamburg, Germany